THE PERFORATED MAP

The Perforated Map

ELÉNA RIVERA

Shearsman Books
Exeter

First published in the United Kingdom in 2011 by
Shearsman Books
58 Velwell Road
Exeter EX4 4LD

http://www.shearsman.com/

ISBN 978-1-84861-160-3

Cover photogravure copyright © Lothar Osterburg, 1999.

Acknowledgements

Grateful acknowledgment is made to the editors of the journals in which some
of the poems in this book first appeared: *The Poker, Aufgabe, Stand Magazine,
Parcel Journal, Tuesday: An Art Project, The Solitary Plover* and *Five Fingers
Review.*

Some poems first appeared as limited-edition chapbooks. Many thanks to
Richard Deming and Nancy Kuhl for publishing *Disturbances in the Ocean of Air*
(New Haven: Phylum Press, 2005), to Guy Bennett for publishing *Suggestions
at Every Turn* (Los Angeles: Seeing Eye Books, 2005), and to Andrea Brady
and Keston Sutherland for publishing *Mistakes, Accidents, and a Want of Liberty*
(Barque Press: Cambridge, 2006). Many thanks to Rachel Moritz and Sun Yung
Shin for publishing *When the Shadow Filled Window Opens* in the WinteRed
Press Chaplet Series. *Disturbances in the Ocean of Air* was first published by
Stand Magazine, Newcastle-upon-Tyne, UK, Winter 1998, Vol. 40, No. 1; it was
First Prize winner, *Stand Magazine* 2nd International Poetry Competition.

The author also wishes to thank Russell Switzer, Denise Newman, the
MacDowell Colony, the Djerassi Foundation and "52 West 91st Street, Apt. 9."

Contents

In us an impulse tests
the unknown

—Lorine Niedecker

The Perforated Map I

Suddenly

on my knees

this large

Bittersweet

pull

Ars Poetica

Inaudible perhaps
this moment, inevitably

washing face and hands
it slips

away, forgotten
by our "progress."

I am drawn to explore aspects,
features of the seen/heard,

which limp still catch light,
colors, twigs of hope.

I slip in your side,
indistinct,

a moistened hand,
a gangling sinew

where the space of the poem
cascades

as years peel one after another
their films of silence.

Bodies encounter effigies
and turn, bloodless, unable

to defend themselves from distance—
the soundless features

of today holds
unwittingly the lineaments

returns the words home,
opens hinges.

Disturbances in the Ocean of Air

1.

Across the border
soft sadness feathers

A blue way
an icy improvisation

2.

Prepare yourself before entering these impervious parts.

> I took a stroll down the corridor and saw
> the Pacific hanging on a clothesline.

> Did my thoughts choose this commotion?
> I wanted to compose under the overpass

> so as not to hear the roar of the city.
> I took off my clothes and slid down in

> a cold, moist repository—
> "and then who knows? Perhaps we will

> be taken in hand by certain memories,
> as if by angels."

3.

The full moon opens a hole overhead, hovers. I am cut open with an
arrow of air. Disturbed by this I start to run. I am running around
in circles of different sizes. Which one will lead to where I want to

go? My head is at the level of my mother's hand. I press my cheek against her soft smooth hand, her "every soft thing." Turbulent pleasure. She says, "A man will go home and tell his family how a little girl kissed his hand in the subway today." That was around the time when I saw the movie *Hara Kiri*. The wooden sword went in with much difficulty.

4.

Tender children
clipped

mad for a home
but only housebroken

5.

I wake from the dream while lunate pleasures adapt to stillness. I hear the sound of my body; it lies supine on the wet bed. I am wearing a wool coat (and nothing underneath). In the distance a truck/jeep is going toward the border of an immense ocean (disorder here). Water moves violently up and down, up and down. If this is real life what can one do? (I think.) If this is fiction what can happen? She is lying on the floor and levitates up and down, up and down, almost banging (terrifying). The way with childhood memories—how things are magnified. I was explaining how I was in a room where something was going on—how I could have taken it wrong, because when the insect crawled on my body it seemed like such a big thing. So in the room with Mom and this man, I could have easily, taken what had happened as a much bigger thing.

6.

Can one imagine: "Desire without the object of desire"?
Without even an image?   an extract?   lava?

7.

Scarlet
Scar

Imagine the peeling bark
of a madrona

What is underneath?
That huge intrusion

8.

A movie can also magnify a drip: *"You didn't see it."* those words *"You didn't hear it."* I was pushed from both sides, put in that in-between place, that bridge—the place between "tree" and "wood," "morning glory" and "dried flower," or "cow" and "a piece of beef wrapped in cellophane."

9.

and then you stumbled across
I was at that age

where I heard everything
a vessel for every hard word

From mouth to air to ear
The line is taut

Words are changed by refraction
Can you rest where it is dark?

The Colors Project I

language creeps   into   snowthoughts   I and my

penchant for   out out damn spot

spiral down   enter the woodpecker   peck peck

at my soft and fuzzy   and the juice runs up the tree

sound it out   a young deer in front crossing   as I came

One stood and stared   watched me   descend

into the cold   place

my heartless branch   I wasn't sure I would go there   yet,

simple but then I had to   I make myself   that's the problem

make myself   She will she will she will

      and "I" stuck   mud, snow, fatigue

        results in nudity   and then the idea of failure

another *moyenne*   no not that not not   compare

the drip drip   the juicy   blotting out   the long

obscure sides of my mouth   give me something to do

before rising   the amethyst   stillness

typographically   drops our day

The Colors Project II

Honeysuckle   sunshine

carves holes in my eyes   soft light wheel   a vans motor

running   A portrait   In the morning   a pump

shutting out bird calls, heaters, refrigerators   We will put you

in an envelope to try your feathers   slip   slip

so you will have to pay close attention   hair bleached

by the sun   what is muddled at first

grows clear   in time   at times   barely

Warm me   and I will bathe   in an essence   of what is left of

       jaune or four syllables in Spanish   spreads

the call to rivers

beaches,   and the children playing with building and the making

of the ephemeral   this is my deep trickle Lorine as we play

call and response   your words   so engrained

     each plump grain has become   cell in me   absorbed

    as we reach   toward the sun   absorbing light

more than we can handle   giving it all   giving what we can

our words   our narrow limits   softening   the hard meeting

the chair   sit bones   coming out of excrement

    and falling back into it to seek sweet suckling

Crossed Out

The written fact (lies) transmitted
and ignored, jewel of red daylight
Words take on meaning and we, carried
heartbreakingly by the speck of possibility

"desire for desire"

the density of that edge
dominates as I bind myself
angry at being rebuffed—
Full of wiles these words

"jewel of red daylight"

that ensnare me,
dominate, as I bind myself
to the density of that edge—
desire rebuffed

   again and again

     these stairs pull

       ice gleams, hold

        the Mind Tower

or "an angry person"

slips out (can't help it)
We contradict,
    slip into
desire dense with specks

all open

        sieve words

           all

              all

The Perforated Map II

the rapture

uncharted

       parts

           disintegrate

              wilderness

expected

Suggestions at Every Turn

Nothing is simple when traveling long distances;
          time gets in the way, and the verb "to be."

There was no room,
words in the way of
rooms, put together
distance, on a string,
and breath a shutter

Shut inside a house,
divided, wheels and
an ocean dirge
Opened at the start
   Changed I
when forcibly taken

                    hole in the clouds

"We now live near the ocean, hardly real, and culture a beating."

What was ruptured
at the beginning, be
at school or at home,
a signature of the times

Branded with Signs

Thought signals an occurrence
we had not expected,
sometimes filled with violence

Superimposing emotion
the signs "Black" "White"
imposed extremes on the child

Looking outward down the street
tentacles toward a glazed look
shut down before mealtime

                                   better stay away
                                   suggests an angry
                                   turn inward

"I saw, by looking down into the street, a very long road to and from . . ."

What matters in a market economy
where apartments are bought
like furniture, when desire brings you
to the edge, in between the crisp sheets
generating a lack of balance
between going out and staying in,
being on top or writing it,
getting dirty or disintegrating

To and from in a liner
money and space
reconstruct the tongue
"I want to go home"
Burns the back, the throat

Rules, though strict, are finally very simple.

A photograph of a family
father, mother, brother, sister,
ruled around a large round table,
backs straight, faces forward
The voyage was undertaken
with sang-froid on the part of some
and molten lava on the part of others
The great urgency of achievement,
given precedence at the slot machine
while the small sit at a window, looking
at the ocean prairie, thinking of sinking
and of all that was lost.

"Now I am sitting
by the window
looking down"

"Somehow 'I' remain outside."

nothing said nothing, no
words of praise remained
for the children waiting—
a station, a dock, a ditch,
an airport the site of flight,
duty-free hell disturbed
nothing on a dark night,
windy night, scary night
In the night wheels go round
The square of time in neon

Whatever one wants in bold green lettering.
      "Pay the price!"
         "Come on in!"
A movie couldn't be smelled, but could shake.

"One Night Only!"
The samurai shook his sword
The woman shook her breasts

These conditions bring about
anguish for the very small,
silent "because we dwell"

Indeed nothing cushioned
or softened the looking
Down stares images start

To untangle the wreck count on one of two things,
 sheer stupidity, or plain hardheadedness.

The pushing heavier than
anything imagined, hardened
surfaces are difficult to turn
round to force All of this praise
in Agitation never quite counted
Disregarded the need for words
in a book tangled threads and smells
of paper and private pictures
arrests development, tagged
on city walls

"Cut me or mold me of whatever you want.

    I'll wear a blue cover or a yellow one, whatever pleases you most."

Agitated heart "She
sitting by the window"
warding off the impulse to break

Beneath our human flesh
Caesura   exigency of glass,
There were others
here in this place, before us
What happened?

The violence we tore into
follows the boredom with
the ruthlessness of sex appeal

That strangeness of plastic
and the "beautiful woman"
Distinction cut from a magazine

"Cut the crap!" "That's how
it's been" "I hear the kick in it,"
"A constant trembling down"

                    littoral scattering

The window soon opened, pages covered, typewritten, a comic picture—

Lemniscate effect

Kafka wrote about it in his story, 'The Burrow.' Dwellings complete and incomplete. Danger and fear above and below. Going down and going up. Hearing things.

Sunken in a living room
an image of that space,
in that building on the corner
where what burned
was the caving in,
the ache of craving

A residence for quakes, at the piano
a notion that if denied a song
existence might be thrown like a dime
a separate "see what will happen"
blurred words

"Let's just hoist ourselves up so that we can live."

From the 9th floor, drop a dime
between pauses, could kill
Thoughts like these enter
the pauses, Lots of pauses
The light of such moments
seen from above the street,
above the enclosed spaces of
tunnels, subways for pedestrians
who ignore the motion,
the body's lulled mention

                              lambent elements

"The shadow of a 'story'" "Leaned forward to test how far" "Leaned forward and dizzy" "Young girl falls to her death and kills"

Life goes from
   limbs, they sink,
      the mouth is sear,
         dry.
           State of
               Suspension
                   in it
                     If your house
                          apartment   were
                             If your room   were

Windows allow for the possibility of falling, looking, breaking.

    Whole lives spent in museums, on shelves, behind windows.

Flash. Flash. "Travel with me"
A moving star, stunned
"Eat it up baby! Obviate my pain."
A soldier going back and forth
between the ship experience,
and the skip experience
Tremors, seasickness, loneliness
A cultured snack for in between

Visitors come, go, but we go nowhere.

Recognizing that this happened,
and accommodating
Reading, something relinquished,
forced a 'you' onto the map
Cognizance of the extruded
Windows sealed the poem,
possible turn toward disaster
mirrored the bonds of vanity
driving the wheels of the chariot

                                        the real

                                        never is

                                        not,

                                        the

                                        possibl

                                        e

                                        outcom

                                        e

                                        is never

                                        given

Nothing changes except the groping.

in new accommodations
"Show yourself!"
The young girl dressing descends in estimation
"Come on smile!" comes the order,
her hair in disorder, bending
"You'll like it," repeated pressing
"Let me show you!" "Don't be a stranger!"

The hand hangs its crushing weight, knots crossing (the texture of them).

"Because bored, because nothing
otherwise." How do we travel
in the old word, odd
world "uncharted"

We are
in this mutual transpiring,
wrestling with wind and light
O sky. O wind. O rain.
Give me a cigarette.

"Dimes fall from pockets, kill numerous passersby, fall from apartment building window."

Unfold the shelves
    silent encounter
        on stark pavements
            of wet stone and blank
                skies, borders icy,
                    faces beat, curbed
                        There's never a simple
                            tucking, Not after the slap,
                                the architecture of strife and
                                    the desert all ice

The wind shook the glass. "It has become unbearable . . . turning
into something that isn't what I was" Something
fallen in that deep green of the cold
"Only if you let it creep in," "Like
death in all these collusions."
The weather had
turned

The Colors Project III

drops of flat rain   a place to join /
withdraw   a mirror where fantasy takes over   the real rests
inside a basket of fruit   nothing touched the painting   I
followed this eruption this different perspective   I collected
coins for a cave   dimes and quarters dimes and quarters
jiggling in your pocket   mine stayed put in my purse /wallet rather
The machine beckons; it's seductive narrowness will never deliver
an apology,   never defend itself, never prove you wrong
a kind of animal   without needs   The needs of others
stones in our bodies   at that hour
where the silver screen inside our cells/pinned on walls, pinned on stars
      stars   stars   stars   stars
    in the mind   stains   stainless steal
     education   we have become a set game, chance/
enslavement mixed in   like a horse trained to carry   trained
to pull and trot and run   my   reputation
an image of the pensive brooder in a negative   a gadfly
called on to replicate over and over the departing conscience

The Colors Project IV

Remember how blue jays used to bother   their cawing insistence
                    children hanging from skirts and pant legs
Color of the iris   amidst the yellows
browns and greens of early spring   I'm not translucent
              that gush a couple of days ago   I kept
hearing her voice   Caw   Caw   the Russian poet
     Caw   Caw   the lineage
Spring rains and dark skies   feathers wide open
              the way   with demons I plant my feet
ground of my own making   small hands grab   meat
          aqua green buds   Nothing to compare it to
formed by counting syllables   We all have to
keep noticing colors   "My blue way"   I called it then
experienced   cool airshaft   piercing center   That
or being squeezed between buildings, in a crowd, *une foule*, like languages
          mesclando se   every time   That
and absence   breath filled   sax
          the whole hole   finally
falls into fits of exhaustion   The substance   entire
fingernails breaking   my voice   the wooing of the inaudible

The Perforated Map III

contemplating

passage through

these parts

by simply molding

one's life story

In the Frame of the Door

Early morning shaking showering the left hand
with a glass full of words cracking the surface
of this site, full of the state I find myself in: trembling
for one word

With a pen in hand, I revisit the burned,
review the past and see how the glass breaks
"remember what it was like to be me"
inhabiting the garden

How I was seen then, empty and open—
In a state of anxiety, sand pours down
the hourglass down the hallway full
of multiple loveliness

"Just as thought is written on the body"
the creature I created with letters of the alphabet
is all sharp edges, painted shapes, odd angles
with a greenhouse exterior

A puzzle gone wild, breaks into shards
that need sorting, not the compulsive worrying
at an entrance of the already present
bewitching interior

The language of the body stings in paradise,
the chosen motion pulls toward the cherries

at the center, sifts through daffodils and churns
the butter's big big book

Something came forward that I hadn't expected,
shaped by early experiences and being stuck
in the souvenir of deep red, brown, purple anger
and frustration

Without someone to listen, without language
"she couldn't enter the moral life"
A frozen mind, unraveling, shaking in the classroom,
a leaf on paper

Standing in that courtyard (you could almost
see through language, into its interior,
that boiling chamber; its nouns and pronouns
revealing absence,

blockading movement) I glimpse the shared
messy intimacy that was scattered by lantern
too bright for "the life of the builder"
and so ghosts

promise a genealogy, soon, and its ripple effect
named in a theatrical dream whose juice
is remembrance, and the burning of the left
an emulsified turn inward

Poem with a Line Drawn Across the Body

1.

The passenger of this tableau
plays with obedience, so ones

thirst, the animal's body-signals,
must become prelude to the gist underlying all

techniques "for getting to know
what is not ourselves."

2.

What the body gets used to,
out of necessity operates

as a reminder of what came before.
The cracking of an oyster.

Anything piercing enough
to penetrate.

3.

The Mind constantly clamorous with noise, leans forward into the freeway of time. The tread on the tires is worn. The action of resistance the only traction. Here the cough drowns out the sounds of the rain in an instant. Pain torqued the curve of the anxious branches and the only thing left to do is to walk in trefoil patterns.

4.

History keeps her rowing—

Pulverized quickly by the quietus
of the group surface, an empire's

smooth exterior scratched on,
gives itself an alibi for its market economy

based on fear; its mechanical brutality.
Will-breaker and barbaric, have you

seen the face of those left behind?

5.

The wounding penetrates deeply during
after the childlike opening of the body—
Fresh advance into the next step,
easing itself into the warm pool.
The steam room opening and clearing
the pores, her parents could have
said those words, "You're so . . ."
The child taking those words into
the inner recesses, the corners, the cracks—
A physical calamity at the cellular level.

6.

On the top of his palm, gravity infinitely
calculated to reach the bottom of the rill—

is his hole   his emptiness   what isn't
How far, how fast can you run from what is?

The truth of human life gained by contact
and carved into the decaying body.

Ancient Greek sculptors tried to avoid that
choosing marble to defray the costs of the dead.

But dying is an art and we do it not so well
injecting inertia itself into encounters

and the city's concave connection
takes place at all levels of exchange.

7.

A WALL/crossed
newspaper barricade,

a crater for the lurid and the suffering—
War in all its different guises

How can the body take all the confrontation?
hostility? the build-up of arms?

Complicit in the personal story is consciousness.
The photograph looms large, testing,

a few coins for a look at that which breaks
some say, reality pushed further and further

into the background battle.
PLAYED AGAINST IT/avoidance

8.

Lungs fill with smoke, filled with—

and the body stands before the camera,

smiling in the midst of wood smoke

for the camera, a flue closed chimney—

Carrying the reprimand with her

for the camera smiles and keeps smiling,

the Mona Lisa gone wild.

9.

Famished fame that vacant
mark mandates the difference

between cities drawn into chalk,
cast to build relief for reliance.

Being seen results only in saying
farewell to the very end—A hand

stand moistens every minute's enigma,
tense with balancing between relations

full absence as he sits on the edge,
his seat eager to speak

the subject's
barbarous sentence.

10.

kept by architects at a distance—
MADE WITH /The man's words

His gruff hand softened by a few hairs,
a gesture over laden with meaning,

sensual and worn, or emotional,
at attention, seeking habitation—

Come close then extend the interplay
of ocean here near before nothing after,

not necessarily a bleak prospect, but
the girl kept trying to build something new.

Watch how the street is crowded with regrets,
the small was immured there,

exchanges are her mark and listen others
fearful those fingers impatient, bored

at the beginning middle and end
force is used to open the field—

Nostalgia before, after and during
War's flatulence fated to become history

bored when someone becomes more
and the little children will scour the streets.

The River, the story of a statue, stately and indifferent
ripped the lines of our "self" to shreds,

a part may collapse but careful "the body
plays a part in all apprenticeships."

When the Shadow Filled Window Opens

For Selah

At that particular point in the day when the sun

becomes a loaf of bread, high enough that I can

open its container and look out of the window,

I keep my gaze directed away from annihilation

and worrying traces of destruction, that abyss

of the self, where character was only conceived

to be joined to, perceived in ignorance or blanketed—

a position that in any case, changes in increments.

The way the meadow observed from my desk

becomes a site for daydreaming, for moving away

from reality. Immensity glimpsed at by just

("just"?) changing ones position. The difference

another makes as to how one hears things,

the way grass follows a path, goes from yellow

to blue to green and one remembers the smell

of it, wiggling ones toes. The blow perceived need

not be a problem, just a way of approaching

a thing, otherwise shadowed by the viewfinder

given (the one I became close to for a while

found that she could comfort me, "Let me

rub your back; it makes me feel better").

The same picture-taking lens shifts our universe

if moved. The trillium endangered, blooms

just at the start of the season. I was told about

what was present and the woman couldn't help

but to cut herself (a maroon colored trillium),

admitted to an "abuse situation" in which cutting

had first occurred, and that she hadn't been able to

help herself, to keep from cutting, until now,

and still everyday she thought of it. A strawberry

heaviness carried too many atoms of thought.

Considered through different lenses I sit

with necessity and allow for interactions,

a pause in all my meandering, by looking

into the oven. Protective thought. My friend

a sparrow, I think. I saw her outside

in the meadow, and from my window I

could see that the place I saw, from the window,

allowed for a breaking point in my own wall.

There was this sensation of the floor being above

ground. What was obscured lay behind the visible.

The desk a place to think quietly, a place

to come into a black fly paradise. In that room,

words backing me into a cell I came to treasure,

I build structures, a great variety of them,

the way the artist built a boulder, to photograph it.

Both needing a great variety of structures,

thought patterns, so that no lack of breath,

no lack of particles need be diminished, regardless

of melancholia. A basic situation with room for all,

where the universe enters in telling the story

or by the circular design of the boulder.

The distances between thought and action

were diminishing, but the war kept being

mentioned in the papers, the deaths, the wounded.

The way this was perceived, first looming

then receding. Between that and this, receding

quickly and letting the planes of thought appear

in a series, instead of as a mirror, melting

what was reflected into itself, mirroring a way

of looking at things from different vantage points

where what was trapped was noticed. Now, the same

today as it is tomorrow, wrote the philosopher.

We are at the center and can't hope to get out.

What was natural to her became immense ocean,

most observations demanded the tiniest looking,

the same huge schemes for discipline proliferated.

The planetary expansion of her mind taking notice

of what she had only previously read about. I spent,

knew that her attention was needed, and the book

would bring her to that from the place at her desk

to the pattern of her poem, from the raised look,

to a moment spent on a three-petal wild flower.

The Perforated Map IV

externals are simply many props in   an

age of media   what

motives inspire   our

struggle?

We Will Be Served

It's true that fury burns boredom
fills the gaps with story and emotion,

a word world distorts the moment's
motion and the hand is hung

dry, the reply—Dommage there's so much
damage, glimpse of the bigger bully

emptying the road side attraction
of it's spacious crepitant calls.

Superhero stamps construct
the flavor of the day, in a face

"under" we say, "Middle Eastern"
eyes toward the sky, toward

the sword ache of word wars,
sidewalk sounds, naming under cover.

Easy to say "indifference" then "aggressive,"
fear claims our "territory" we say,

desperate names are pinned to a cushion—
"What should *I* call ..." these links, wings,

my feet because generations wait
for this play gripped by its naming.

What country have "I" entered? Narrative
captures the attention "where *I'm* going"

or "What I *hold*" reaping the benefits
of hours turned into cash, into games, into. . .

Listen to the words as a lyricist would;
is it enough? Turn the page, keep moving,

Overhead: Thought planes.
                        Who says we won?

Clowns, masks, broken dolls, disaster,
objects "left behind when someone goes

away or dies." Dommage there's so much
damage, moving into nothingness,

"saved" from identifying, and empty—
"spared" we say, boredom's terrible tray.

Mistakes, Accidents, and a Want of Liberty

"thinking of my life, I almost forgot my liberty"

Ah tentative road, you open a sense
of wrongness! Passing for a face, a passport,
crowds of people crowd—a beggar I
move through this broken naught.

Forsake the name, birth will build bone
the structure of the precautionary impaled
in traffic, in countless trials of geography,
ground by the body's explanation.

I reach, uncertain of my wildest fuchsia,
forgotten ecstasy in that foreign territory.
Perhaps I swallow to survive the ripe
reasons shortening my threadbare existence.

Whose words but my own, in a silence
that levels the rooms of freedom as I face
the wall of my own lack of sweetness.
Pining for attention I almost forgot . . .

I almost forgot

The quality of a question when asked
whether one would rather have a hammer,
length or meaning. The quality of the
mechanism that manifests the toolbox.
The quality of a tale when it turns into
an investigation, into glue, paint, pencil,
pliers. The ruler underlines all. Robes
of sound knock on the "most unhappy."

The most unhappy

Return of a soldier met
strangeness. In the city who
takes the time to understand
the condition which was.
Reluctance at first to
speak devastation then
tickets bought words a
poster these scarlet shots.

Snapshots best express
disappearing the what.
Will the image help hold
the style of certain. We
made slaves to this of
our depressed mind (so
carry the sign) "Damage"
not just a thing of the 30's.

Peacetime arguing cold
in rain about the leash.
Blow winds and crack
the dog that man tied not
to "post-modern" scrawls
but unhook rivalries from
weary wreckage, sharp jeers
and "violent green space."

Green

The relation between a buyer and his money—
A manifestation of "I" and "Mine"
ingested. The evidence of what was used up.
(Hesitant at first then filled with aphorisms.)
An assertion of the mark absorbed into the silhouette
so that the "real" (we are convinced) was squandered
(something for which we trade our lives).

Our lives

subservient patchwork structure
I, you, we, us
crushed alive

"It's not a competition; it's war."
TV & papers report
distill alarm

Billboards bear the surface
with shock
"devastating"

wrangles the advertisement
replete with adjectives
glued to the drama

To such "one way" convictions
add pills to contain
opinions

At the climax
a supine scene
"see"

See

The limit of reproduction and replica,
of "you" as reflection, of "you" as reaction,
of the quest of enough, not enough,
when will there be enough, next time,
what time, the countless ways waste
makes assumptions, especially at the
juncture of joining labor with libation.
Greater than, lesser than, the equation
of product equals trash equals trade,
acquires pattern, assails this subject, taints

Subject

I am ready to trace the translation
from stone to snow fingers cramped
around a line drawn in air by the poet
of dark skies in a white season.

The sedulous may yet see the sun
pundits tell us. Our simple response
to history is to rearrange the ashes.
The composite is terrified by the tearing.

The lacerations "opened my eyes"
to the "horrible pit" & "no ladder upon which
to get out." I wear the pliable robes,
the physical rules of a strange country.

A strange country

Expectations demand a gentle price, the robes
of the subordinate. Embedded in the process
of covering and wrapping is a manifestation
of the whole. Suppose the family crown is worn
by all that deserve it, would you wear it then?
Part of the issue at stake here is if you ask yourself,
more than once, to surround yourself with explosions
would you survive? Would you find the happiness
you seek amidst such pomp and hilarity? The mouth
opens wide for an answer then closes again in
expectation of a different question.

Different

The length of the moored body
a corridor of twine
today's question.

Under the lash,
under the exercise
of comparison,
crimson wales develop.

Excision has meaning for the numerous.
The number of stones lifted
turn
homecoming into danger.

Families conceal
a shrouded empty heaviness
of sound.

A stranger negative,
ourselves
ashen and swimming,
painting our evidence.

Painting our evidence

A blue frame measures the family outing.
An investigation into the "brutalizing effects"
between what you have, what I have, and
the measuring of a "wretched condition,
without remedy."

(A hole grows at the center and water
Doesn't fill it, even if you dive in.)

The comic book version destroyed all
possibility for heroic action. Desensitized
to travel, the fluctuations of mind turn
into a habit. If you "seek domestic fury"
you will find it. Take a plane instead,
be valiant, keep your lines taut, tenacious
reverence demands shameless
superfluous tripping.

Shameless

plastic & silver walls
manufactured

              for our use

facts
on loan

              Ruled

in a reoccurring season
Note

              the knock

stumble
into expenditure

              Investigate

air
medium-rare and thick

              with constructs

brazen
into someone else's

              err

Err

We are spent, mistake me not. We restless and ruled
beggars, a good dog, "till I became my own master."
Rulers of nothing, it turned out (heard that tune
more than I'd care to). Commend me to my inheritors.
A rude way. Winter reckons with politics and ensures
dimes, quarters, and bills—buy up my merchant's woe.
The buyer chooses his suit like a song, pinstriped
tales shall get, whereas solids shall lose, unless mended.
The difference between blues, "a slave in fact" and
"a slave in form," and a thrifty command will tax you.
A woman sits, folds her arms and whispers so that
everyone can hear, "All I know is the alphabet!"

The alphabet

At the axis, our parts expressed,
the real wrapping transparent,
our "robes" given up as scrap.

My destiny brought me here,
bought me a scrap, two shames,
one island behold brute sheaf.

I land in red language scarves,
silk scraps on a fractured lens
of a subdued design.

In the arranged shipment, liquid
covenant, constrained by the fault,
the dust, the informed brush of a scarf.

A mantle covers the ship, covers
the question about the mechanism,
about the "I" brushed in a series.

We are wooed by the city's setting ways—
I resolved to knock things down.
Interwoven reflections of sounds.

The Colors Project V

a body   stretched out   in the building's entrance
      needle in arm   around the ground   nearby
needles to prick   picked and dropped   more than just hair
air turns   walk   trying to avoid the hurtling
words, insinuations, come-ons, into the bodega for a pack of cigarettes
into   walk   the right coin amount not
   five flight of stairs   walk   into the pale building   not fatigued
        walk   into the small gray room   light
a cigarette   mattress on the floor   walls   a dark
gray sheen   pigeon light   in this place there is no
beginning or end, only a middle   middle of the road   middle of
the threshold   gray cover and black bold lettering   The body
    emptied   filled   inebriated   impoverished
    pushed into   Mauled   and man-handled
"making it"   The news is bad   Desire burns
but kept at bay   Books cite warnings   Inertia roams free
   The clock grows stamens   The crowding
    solitude of the hours   crowds

The Perforated Map

Suddenly

on my knees

this large

Bittersweet

pull

the rapture

uncharted

     parts

        disintegrate

          wilderness

expected

contemplating

passage through

these parts

by simply molding

one's life story

externals are simply many props in   an

age of media   what

motives inspire   our

struggle?

To be true to that   that too is a

deed   behind the ears, down

the spine, the arch of the foot

watch

the spectacle

wait

until the words grow

Pieces

fall

                        daily

at each interval

forced to face oneself

still a bright seed

just as real

dans n'importe quel langue

The adder in my path

bit me

so that I fell

Forced back by ice   into

a wall

suffering is always with us

does it matter what form it takes?

behind the blow

"the known and unknown

touch"

I shall no longer flirt with words

cerulean insight

in   the   same   bare   place

remote

destination   a small line

from time to time

Map   out   the   source   of   panic

familiar

tension

Our generation

grieves

immobilized by the urge

to yield

let me

bear it   well

the great and

sore

s c o r c h e d

surface

inside us

all

Asked

about

the eventual

the "eternal"

my legacy

bound

around

Hunger

rescue my space

the land

once

marked

pierces

the mirror face

unmistakable

we have to find it   the

threshold

when it comes

(bewildered

by possible obscurity)   the everyday

apocalypse

Departing meant

a place

to go

the image of ourselves

open

mouthed

Notes

p. 15: "and then who knows? Perhaps we will be taken in hand by certain memories, as if by angels." is by Marguerite Yourcenar

p. 17: "Desire without the object of desire" is from Wallace Stevens, *The Collected Poems*

p. 36: "The shadow of a 'story'" is from 'The Story of It' by Henry James

p. 42: *The weather had turned* is from 'The Story of It' by Henry James

p. 50: "for getting to know what is not ourselves" is from *Memoirs of Hadrian* by Marguerite Yourcenar

p. 56: "The body plays a part in all apprenticeships" is from *Waiting for God* by Simone Weil

p. 66: "thinking of my life, I almost forgot my liberty" is from *The Narrative of the Life of Frederick Douglass: An American Slave* by Frederick Douglass

p. 72: "opened my eyes" "horrible pit" "no ladder upon which to get out" is from *The Narrative of the Life of Frederick Douglass: An American Slave* Frederick Douglass

p. 75: "wretched condition, without remedy," is from *The Narrative of the Life of Frederick Douglass: An American Slave* by Frederick Douglass

p. 77: "till I became my own master" is from *The Narrative of the Life of Frederick Douglass: An American Slave* by Frederick Douglass

p. 92: "the known and unknown touch" is by George Oppen